Mental

Interlude

Mind Flow Publishing & Production LLC
Presents

Mental

Interlude

By DaKiara

First Printing: 2018

ISBN 978-1732243316

Additional copies of this book and others are available by mail or by emailing the listed below.

Mind Flow Publishing & Production LLC
PO Box 48768 Cumberland, North Carolina 28331-8768
Or email at: mindflowpubpro@gmail.com

Cover Art by Miss Web Designer, LLC

**DEDICATED TO MY ANGELS
DAQUAN, DEJA, DANTE
KEVONN AND KIARA**

**RIP
DAQUAN JAMIQUE 95
&
KIARA DENISE 00**

Special Thanks
To GOD for Giving Me
The Strength and The Words
To Do This Project.
Blessed by The Experiences to Draw From
It Has Not Always Been Easy.

To All of My Family
And My Friends
Who Have Stood by Me
During the Duration of This Project
I LOVE YOU…
Without Your Help and Encouragement
I Would Not Have Taken This Step
I Can Not Say THANK YOU Enough
I Hope It Was Worth the Wait
It's Been A Long Time in The Making
So, THANK YOU AGAIN TO THOSE WHO KEPT
PUSHING!!!!! (PUSH…SPLAT…)

A Glimpse into The Author……

DaKiara The Author & Poet was born in Richmond Virginia but grew up in rural Laurinburg North Carolina. She was raised by her mom Dorothy Merriman McNeill along with other influences from the church community. DaKiara is the youngest of three children. She has two older brothers Lee and Lamont. When her mother remarried(Chauncey) she gained two sisters and another brother (Kim, Cierra, and Ernest). She is a wife and a mother to three children and two angels (DaQuan and Kiara). Her writing journey began early in life around age 12 to escape and convey her feelings and those of others around her that couldn't seem to find a voice of their own. Throughout the years she has used her writings to express her love, and her pain of losing two of her children, the state of the world, and just about life in general. For years her writings were her therapy and now she is using it in hopes to inspire or motivate others. With her children (Jacqueline, D'ante, Kevonn) all in college and her herself returning two years ago, she decided to follow her passion and with the help of her husband of twenty-one years Kenny and host of family and friends (92Strong) she is breathing life into her heart's labor. Her writings have expanded from just poetry to now include short stories as well. Her hopes are that people will feel they are not alone in what they feel or go through in their day to day experiences. This is DaKiara's reintroduction into the world and she is excited to take you on her journey. Stay tuned, the best is yet to come.

This Book is Meant to Take You on an Emotional Roller Coaster, Please Strap in and Enjoy the Ride…… DaKiara

Table of Contents

A Mother Weeps

Awaken in the night
But not by dawns early light
Instead from the fright
Something not quite right
Memories flood your mind
Memories you can never leave behind
Peace of mind
Is what you must find
A precious life taken in her sleep
Into the night death creeps
A mother left to weep
As her baby girl sleeps
Why my baby?
Ever think maybe
There is a plan that has been laid
A plan that can't be swayed
Just as the outcome can't be waived
The child played a part
A very important role
You feel it within your soul
So, mother your story must be told
A mother's worst fears come to light
Why did her child die during the night?
A mother's sleepy eyes stood watch
Never in a million years could she see
The coming of this reality
Just another of life's tragedies
A mother gives all her love and care
To hesitate she wouldn't dare
On this day
A mother's nightmare is born
So many questions
Unanswered they go
Her precious one, breathes no more

A Mother's Heart

A mother's heart knows
The heart of her child
A mother's heart can tell
When her child is sick
Or up to some ole tricks
Her heart can tell
If her child has found trouble
She can handle it on the double
A mother's heart knows
Her child's deepest woes
Could be as simple as stubbing their toes
A mother's heart knows
When her little one has been upset
By someone showing disrespect
A mother's heart knows
Her child's deepest fears
Having wiped so many tears
Throughout the crucial years
A mother's heart knows
The heart of her child

A Mothers Love for Her Children is Amazing……DaKiara

A Prayer Answered

Once before you said that sometime ago
You prayed for me
You asked the lord to place
Me within your path
So now here I am
Now that I am here
How will you show me you care?
You told the Lord that you would cherish me
So, will you stand behind your promise?
You asked the lord to send you someone
Who would take you to new heights
You wanted someone to teach you
Teach you to love
Instead of you doing the teaching
Do I meet your expectations?
You wanted someone to show you
That they care
You wanted to feel loved Is your appetite yet fulfilled?
You asked that someone take you by the hand
And walk with you from there.
You prayed for me
So here I am
Has your prayer been answered?

A New Me

Have you ever noticed?
Every year you say to yourself
"It's all about me"
Well this year is my year
It's going to be a new me
Tear free
Drama free
Going to finally tell you
Just how I feel
And let you know this love is real
Going to finally do things
For me
To show the appreciation of myself
Instead of relying upon others to do it
I'm going to get fit
You know we always got to
Try to get that body right
Yes, this is my year
It will be all about me
A new me
At least until I wake up
And then my reality
Takes its place
It's never about just me
The new me or old me

Cold feet

As I stand before you
Looking into your eyes
I've always loved your eye color
A soft tender brown
Kind of subtle not harsh at all
My gaze drops to your lips
So full, so soft
And so sweet upon mine
In my heart I know that you love me
Just as I love you
But try telling that to those nerves
Within my stomach
As if on cue you grab my hand
And give me a look like
"Bae it's going to be okay"
And then a gentle squeeze
As you say your vows to me
I can tell, that you also
 Are trembling within
And it's not just me with the jitters
As you finish you whisper into my ear
"Bae it's going to be okay"
And just like that
I am okay

Emotional Roller Coaster

At times I feel elated just being in your presence
Other times I feel bombarded by your essence
Usually I'm enchanted by your demeanor
Then others I'm feeling as if I'm the meaner
From one moment to the next
I never know what to expect
With you my days are never the same
Sometimes it almost feels as if it's some silly game
One minute I'm on cloud nine
The next I just want to whine
I tell you from experience
And it's not for the sake of appearance
But you keep me on an emotional rollercoaster
Temperatures rise as if I'm in a roaster
One things for certain this ride
Can most certainly not be denied.
My rollercoaster is spinning high
High into the sky
Emotions running wild
Happy one moment
Sad the next
Anxiously awaiting the next ride

Lifetime

It seems as if it's been a lifetime
Since you asked me to be your wife
Although the road hasn't always been easy
We've managed to struggle through it
It seems as if we've grown apart at times
But, then I realize that we have just grown
Sometimes you make me so happy that I cry
And other times
I just cry
You see we have made it through
Some pretty rough times
But, here we both stand
Continuing through the test of time
At times I know you want to give up
And for some blessed reason you still show up
Never throwing in the towel
Always letting me know that it's me you love
Together we have conceived five beautiful children
All extensions of ourselves
They have always been our blessings
Even when we were too blind to see it
Then there was our loss
Of two precious angels
Again, we did it
Together we made it through
It seems like a lifetime ago
That we began this journey
But there is still a lifetime ahead

Mesmerize

Mesmerized by your presence
Captivated by your very essence
Intrigued by your style
Enticed by your smile
Inspired by your intellect
Never confused by regret
Stimulated by your imagination
Motivated by your inspiration
Energized by your fire
Aroused by your desire
Provoked by your mentality
Awakened by your personality
Simply put Mesmerized

Take My Hand

Through good and bad times
I want to be there
To help tow the line
Can I be the one
You lean on?
I want you to feel
As if you have been reborn
By the strength of our love
A love so nice and sweet
Only you can make my life complete
Halfway is where we shall meet
Together we shall walk from there
Embracing the world without a care
Please take my hand

My Mother

For as long as I can remember
From January to December
My mother has been my strength
She has made it through
More rough times than just a few
With three children to raise
I must sing her praise
Our life was never easy
But the good things in life never are
Good and bad memories aren't too far
From my thoughts
I guess in a way it helps keep me grounded
I think we have all become well rounded
My mother has been my strength
When I was weak
No matter what
I know she is always there
Quick to let you know she care
Also, quick to put you in your place
I remember a few times she had to chase
Us to prove her point
She taught us how to appreciate
The little things in life
And to know that we shall always
Encounter strife
It goes back as deep as our bloodlines
But it also helps to define
Who we are
And how we have made it thus far
My mother has been my strength
Through some of my weakest moments
So, I write this as a tribute to you
And all Mothers like you
Which I hope to be someday

Always know
I love you
You've made me strong
And I know that I can carry on
Thanks to you
My Mother

Dedicated to 2 Great Women!
Dorothy A. McNeill & Sheila H. Livingston

I Love You Both for Creating Me
DaKiara

Pain

Pain comes in many forms
There can be mental anguish
Emotional distress
Physical agony
No matter what your pain
It's how you handle your pain
That makes a difference
The key is to use your pain
To nurture your spirit
And to build from it
Don't let your pain overtake you
And control who you become
And how you live your life
Will you succumb to your pain?
Or will you rise above it
Will you welcome the lessons?
To be learned from it
Or will it simply
Manifests itself into more pain
And anger
How will you choose to deal with
Your own pain?

Life

Life can be rewarding
It can also be filled with tragedy
You can find someone to make it fulfilling
Or they may bring you heartbreak
One thing remains true
Your life just wouldn't be your life
Without you
Just when you feel your life is rough
Just buckle down and get tough
Too often bad things happen
To good people
Trust in your heart and rely on your
Family and friends to get you through
It's unfortunate that people
Who feel they are closest to you
Will never know what all
You have been through
The good the bad
The highs the lows
Your life can be filled with grief
Or perhaps just misery
The key is to make the best
Of all situations
Through life you will meet
All different types of people
Some set on harming you
Some that will ultimately charm you
Some who will use
And often try to abuse
Life can be rewarding
Are you open to accept yours?

The Lady

I've seen many women and men alike
Fall to their knees
When the lady takes hold
It's like she gets inside their soul
Sucking away at their essence
Altering their presence
Changing their appearance
Draining the very life from them
Just to have her for a moment
They will lie, steal and cheat
Perhaps even kill
Just to get that one quick thrill
For one short ride
They will be taken to the far side
She is strong
And won't be denied
Once she has her claws within
It's a battle that few will win
Beware of "The Lady"
She comes in many forms
Manifests to what your heart desires
I've seen many men and women alike
Fall to their knees
When the lady takes control

Forbidden Love

Sometimes in life
You are fortunate to find your mate
But, what if that love was forbidden
Whether by beliefs
Or what if by race
Would you go against
All that you believe
Know and trust
To make the most
Of this forbidden love

Sometimes in life
You must make a stand
Follow your heart
And fail you it will not
A love so wondrously true
How could it be forbidden?
You fight against family
You fight against friends
And in the end
You hope and pray
That love wins

That is that Forbidden Love……DaKiara

The "L" Word

So much emphasis is put on one little word
A word that carries so much weight
A word not to be taken lightly, nor slurred
A word that often temps fate

The word can mean many things
There are different levels of intensity
Once said it will feel as if you're flying on wings
And now altered is your destiny
Once the word has been spoken
The relationship is taken to a different place
Because it's been said and given as a token
Of hopes for a new pace
Emotions will begin running wild
You'll feel as if you're spinning without control
Feeling just as wide eyed as a child
Knowing that for them you would give your soul

So much emphasis is put on one little word
A word that carries so much weight
A word not to be taken lightly, nor slurred
A word that often temps fate

This Word Holds a lot of Power…...DaKiara

The Crush

Not quite sure how it started
All I knew is I never wanted it to end
From afar I admired you
Secretly of course
Never imagining that I would
Work up the nerve
To ever approach you
I was content with my stolen glances
And when you smiled
I imagined you were smiling at me
I often daydreamed of you and me
Getting married, having kids, and
Growing old together
Oh, how sweet that would be
One day my thoughts were interrupted
A scent tantalized my nose
It was your own personal scent
It tingled my toes
Then it seemed you looked
Right through me into my soul
For at that moment I could have
And surely would have died
But, I would have died oh so happy
You slid me a note
It simply read
I've got a crush on you
I was too through

Vows

On this day I pledge to you
My love forever will be true
No matter what our lives may bring
It is for you, my heart will sing
A new journey will start
From you, I will never part
When you asked me to be your wife
It truly changed my life
From this day onward
Our lives will move forward
I promise to always share
And you will always know I care
I will be your strength
At your weakest times
I will provide my shoulder
When you need to lean
I pledge my undying love
Just as pure as a white dove
When you came into my life
You stole my heart
Right from the start
Never once have you forsaken me
Instead you just let me be
I love it when you hold me near
And gently kiss away my fear
I know what I feel is right
So, at this time
I would be proud to be your wife

Dear Father

It's really amazing
How this world works
It seems for as long as I can
Recall
I've longed for you
But at the same time
I've come to terms
And realized that
It's a possibility that
It may never be
You see as a little girl
 All my friends had
What I believed was the
Complete family
And I felt somewhat left out
Because I didn't quite fit in
I soon realized that
I must not need you
Because I truly never had you
So, what was I really missing?
I decided long ago
That I would be someone
To be proud of
And I would make it
And here I stand
Still somehow
Needing my Father
Or should I say
Wanting my Father
Wanting his love
His approval
But at the same time
I realize
I don't need it, I want it…

Mind Flow

So much upon my mind
But where to begin
A way I must find
To release what's within
Many thoughts flowing
Got to get my mind going
Looking deep inside
Wanting my mind to take me on a ride
Take me on a journey to find
What's deep within my mind
All around me chaos and havoc
A single thought I must grab it
Just one to get my wheels turning
This is what my hand is yearning
My fingers are ready to find the beat
Never an easy feat
But, once I get started
It's always sweet
So, as I take my seat
My mind is stimulating heat
As my fingers find the beat
My mind has found its starting point
It's finally time to rip this joint

One of My Favorites……DaKiara

You've Captured My Heart

Sitting here in a daze
Thinking of the ways
My boo shows me love
A love so perfect
It must be
From heaven above
It's your simple way
The small things like
Asking me "How was your day?"
Or when you say
"Hi sweetheart."
A love so sweet
Right from the start
Somehow in this short time
You've captured my heart

Writer's Block

I've got so much to say
But can't find the words
So much madness going on
In the world,
But I can't find my voice
Children dying, mother's crying
Still my page is empty
An innocent child has been slain
A mother weeps with pain
Still my page is empty
Sitting back, I clear my thoughts
Then all at once
Multi thoughts overthrow my mind
Taunting me
Still my page is empty
I just need one clear thought
Searching my mind for one single title
To get me started
That's all that's needed
Still my page is empty
A bank is robbed
Two brothers were involved
Still my page is empty
I've got so much to say
Why can't I find the words?
 Every day is full of drama
I must have got hold to some bad karma
Because still my page is empty

The Writer's Struggle…...DaKiara

Within

Far too often we don't take the time
To look and see the person within
We are so quick to jump in
Based off only the superficial
We never take the time
To look deeply into the eyes
To see what a person is really made up of
To find out what makes that person
Who they are
What makes them smile?
Laugh, or even cry
What stimulates their mind?
So next time
Please take the time
To find the person within

What I Want from You!!!!

What I want from you
Can't be simply told
Or even asked
It has to be given
But for me, I feel
I have nothing to give
So, the real question is not
What Do I want from you?
It would be simply
What do I want from me?

Without You

This question that runs through your mind
I have answered from time to time
Will I leave you?
The answer remains the same
My love I can't be without you
With obstacles constantly blocking our path
I truly understand your concern
But with growth I have learned
To walk away from true love
Would be a terrible mistake
Before you for many years
I've often ran when it seemed too hard
So afraid of a broken heart
Without you?
Is not an option in my life
Yes, it is when true frustration
Takes its place
Leaving me to wonder about our fate
But even with all the wondering
That seems to fill my days
I still know that it's worth the wait
Without you?
I will not know the potential of our love
That alone I cannot give up
No one said it would be easy
Not you, not me
To leave you what would I gain?
Why would I search again for love I've already claimed?
Our love is now branded
In a place that is sacred
Did I say that we would make it?
The answer just to clarify
I won't make the mistake of being
Without you

True Love

Mesmerized by the person that you are
Envisioning our union as I gaze afar
Engulfed by the way that you love
Knowing that I am the fortunate one
Never realizing that I could succumb
To love in the unlikeliest of places
But never to question the goodness of his graces
 For in this short time that we have united
There is one thing that I am sure of
 Not often in this lifetime
Will two people find that special connection
That includes honesty, trust, and respect
The three keys that compose true love
 Spiritually and emotionally we have a bond
Never to be replaced by anyone
True love has rescued me
And now as I sit by the side of the sea
Gazing at the stars above the trees
True love resides within me

Dedicated to the One I Love…...DaKiara

The Wait

All my life I've seen you
For years, I have felt you
I knew we would one day meet
The hard part was weeding through the false loves
Now that was no easy feat
So many times, I thought
For sure true love I had found
But those loves quickly died
Sometimes just as quickly as the changing of the tides
To my dismay,
Some loves had longevity,
But they too lost my attention
The day is finally here
That blessed day, we shall meet
Just as I've imagined,
You're all that I never knew I needed

Thoughts

Many thoughts fill my head
Some at times I dread
Some are filled with thoughts of happiness
Many are of marital bliss
But then at times some are of sorrow
Making me not want to see tomorrow
Then I think of you
And all that we have made it through
And I know with you all things can come true
You keep my would be grey skies blue

The Poem

The poem starts out on an empty page
As the writer looks for words
An attempt to express his very
Thoughts
And tell them to the world
As he searches deep within himself
To bring his visions out
The struggle of the writer's pen
A fight within no doubt

So many things have crossed his mind
The events of each new day
As he tries to articulate
The proper words to say
What will he write?
What will he say?
How deep must his thoughts go?
Before him lays an empty page
The process is slow

With each new line
With each new word
His paper no longer blank
A few more lines, one more new thought
I'm almost there he thinks
And as he finishes with this one
Another he must write
The struggle of the writer's pen
He's in for another fight

The Life of a Writer, The Struggle is Real…...DaKiara

The Day

My day began with such promise
Started with a simple kiss
To the lips, and then to the forehead
Your feelings you never spoke
But, from the strength and passion
Of your embrace
I felt every ounce of your love
As the day progressed, I lay
Within the confinements of your arms
I was content to remain there
I told you that your wish
For today would be my command
You said you were hungry
I quickly complied
Presented you with some fruit
You said you were thirsty
Again, I complied
And furnished you with drink
You began to drink in my very essence
The day ended just as it had begun
With such promise for a great future

Another Favorite……DaKiara

Stolen Glances

I look upon your face
Taking in your features
From the distinctiveness of your chin
To the solemnness within your eyes
I look upon your frame
From the strength of your upper body
To the perfect bowing of your legs
All the while I am taking
Stolen glances of you
You never notice me
 I see the way your lips curl
As you smile
I can see the twinkle of joy
In your eyes
And when you laugh
I see the
Strength of your jaw line
All the while I am taking
Stolen glances of you
You never seem to notice me

This Still Holds True……DaKiara

Father's Day

Father's Day is a day of celebration
To celebrate the men in our lives
For being the men that they are
And taking responsibility for the children
They helped to create
This includes being there for them
Through thick and thin
Happy moments as well as those
Not so happy
Being there to witness the
Day to day joys
As well as their pains
Making soup when they are sick
Telling them a bed time story
Maybe just a simple hug
 Stopping to say "I love you"
Those little things mean so much
To your child
So, to you on Father's Day
I applaud you and your efforts
For you have done what so many
Haven't been able to
And that is to step up to the challenge
And come out on top
So once again
Happy Father's Day
On this day you are honored

D'ante

In your short life
You have been through so much
I see within you
Your strength
Although I know at times
You don't
I see within you
Your weakness
This you often see
My wish for you
Is to touch on
Your inner strength
And let your mind go free
Your spirit is that of a
Creative mind
And I know without
A doubt you will be fine

So Proud of You and All That You Do

DaKiara

Deja

You are my second born
Hence the name "Deja"
You are my déjà vu baby
For almost 8 months I carried you
I often wondered what you would be like
What would your strengths be?
Who would you look like?
And surprisingly you were
All that I could have ever imagined

From early on you were strong willed
I could tell your sweet nature
I often could see hints of
Your nurturing side
You would be the little me when needed

I often thought to myself
Would I be strong enough to teach you?
How to be self sufficient
Would you learn how to be a woman?
A young lady with manners
Or would I fail you

After 9 years I see
Hints of the young woman
That you will become
And I am proud to say
You are all I could ever
Want in a daughter
And it is my privilege and honor
To be your mom…………

Truly honored……. DaKiara

Moment Captured

What's the best way to capture a moment?
Simply someone trying to vent
Would it be to put it in writing?
What if it was someone fighting
What about putting it on paper
Telling of how someone caught the vapor
What if someone fell from a skyscraper?
How to capture the moment
An artist mind must use common sense
And always keep the reader in suspense
What if a drunk driver caused an offense?
See how the situation became tense
What is the best way to capture a moment?
A single moment in time
The best way by far is to use your own mind

Worried

To ask if I'm worried
Is truly the understatement of the year
Never in my life have I known such fear
Not knowing if we shall survive
I know you have to feel the vibe
So powerful, so overwhelming
Your friends try to tell you
"No, don't do it"
But you know in your heart
You have to prove it
Will we stand the test of time?
Will our love prevail at the end of this rhyme?
I ask you to please don't turn away
Instead I beg of you to please stay
Right here beside me
That's right for the world to see
That our love is true
If they only knew
The way I make you writhe and scream
And from your eyes tears stream
Tears of joy
This love we have to explore

Source of My Dreams

My dreams began and end with you
I go to sleep with you on my mind
And I awake within your arms
As I close my eyes
I see you and I
In my dreams anything is possible
One thing will always remain true
Not one of my dreams is missing you
You are always and have always
Been that one constant in my life
With you I know and feel that
Any and all things are possible
For you are the source of my dreams
In my dreams and in my reality
You stand by me
You listen and seem to share my dreams
Or so it seems
But nonetheless you are the source of my dreams

She Grew Up Too Early

Gina is a young lady of only fifteen years
But to look upon her face
You would swear she's much older
Having already had a nice share
Of boo's
Having experienced intimacy at the
Tender age of twelve
She began getting these urges
These feelings
She began feeling the tingling
Within her body at the sight
Of an attractive young man
The boys began to notice
How mature she looked
And they began to compliment her
This only added to her curiosity
So, it was nothing
When the first asked her
If he could get a little taste,
Or perhaps catch a feel
But Gina couldn't stop with just that

He wanted to go further
So, she allowed it.
Soon word got around
That Gina was active
And pretty soon another was trying
To get a bit, and then another
Now at the tender age of fifteen
Gina is faced with a new challenge
How to raise a child
When she is still just a child herself
Her mother tried to warn her
As well as most others
Gina is just another little girl
Who grew up too early
Now she has the weight of the
Innocent child upon her shoulders

So Many Innocent Children Lives are Disrupted at an
Early Age……. DaKiara

Quest for True Love

Many have searched for true love
But what is this?
What is true love?
This often evades most
And usually when we find this
We never seem to notice
So is true love,
Finding that one you're most
Compatible with
The one you share your
Darkest secrets
The one who always
Listen to your every word
The one who shares
Your hopes and dreams
The one who lifts you up
When you're at your lowest
Could it be the one
Who always seems to make you
Smile
Who makes your face light up
Like the sunrays
Or is it that one who just seems
To be there
And always show you they care
Making the little things
Seem like so much
Tell me
On your quest for true love
What have you discovered
Is the key?

Puzzle

Imagine if you will
A puzzle

Beautiful as it is when fully constructed
The pieces fitting perfectly
Each one intertwining with the next

Now, imagine if you will
You and your soul mate

Beautiful you two are when put together
The two of you fitting perfectly
Your bodies intertwining with each other

What would happen if you lost a piece
To your puzzle?
The whole thing would be worthless
The same could be said
If you lose a piece of your soul
My life without you is worthless

Wings

I watched as you spread your wings
I watched as you began your flight
I watched as you did it with all your might
I sat back and watched you crawl
I sat back and watched you fall
I proudly watched as you took a stand
and finally became your own man
As a parent, it is my job to protect you
As often as the world tries to reject you
As I sit back and watch you take flight
You vanish from my sight

Exposure

My mental is on a level not many can reach
Don't mean to seem conceited, simply here to teach
I was brought up in a world of love and compassion
Now all around me I see people harassing
Others because they are different
This only makes them feel insignificant
What will it take, for people to see
Inside you are the same as me
How many lives will be lost
What is the final cost
The debt needs to be paid
A new path laid
We are all sisters and brothers
Why must we see colors
We all bleed and cry
We all are freed when we die
From the life we chose
When we die, our lives are truly exposed

Tribute to Parkland

17 innocents shot, slain
who is to blame
is it the one
who shot the gun
is it the one
who chose to walk
as the child
tried, begged to talk
children's bodies laying everywhere
so many people, pretending to care
all the screams turn to silence
all the while the violence
never cease
instead we are left with more deceased
too many children dying
too many souls are crying
when does the madness end
or is it just the beginning
of a world with no end

My Prayers to the Families That Were Affected…. In Actuality
We All Should Have Been Affected in Some Form. Human Lives
Were Lost…. Enough is Enough…...DaKiara

The Corners of Your Mental

Close your eyes and allow me to explore
Promise once I'm done
I will leave you begging for more
Deep inside
Where no other has ever ventured
I happily brave the uncharted territory
Loving the thought
I'm the first who has sought
To know you on this level
So much wonder and amazement
As the corners of your mental
Are touched for the first time

I Hope You Are Enjoying the Ride So Far……DaKiara

Getting Back on Track

What do you do when you have a secret love
But even your secret love seems to have a secret
Shall we dare say love
Just the thought, my blood became super-heated
But wait, I have no right to be mad
After all it was a gamble we both partook
I will admit, it had me a bit sad
Tears I shed, the feelings I mistook
But now I'm bouncing back
Getting my life on track
No more of that veering off course
Taking control of my life back with sheer force

My Moon

If I had to label you
As an object
I would label you
Simply as my moon
Not as my sun
Because, that would be
Too bright,
You my love are much softer
Not as my raindrops
Because they only come
In spurts
You my love are a constant
You would be my moon
You would be my strength
To get me through the darkness
Because of your strength others
Will always pale in comparison
You are my moon

My Love Letter to You

My love
As we walk through this life together
Heart to heart, hand in hand,
And soul to soul
There will be so much to experience
So much for me to see through your eyes
And for you to see through mine
I'm filled with anticipation of what our life will bring
No need for materialistic things
Such as diamond rings
No, our love is worth much
More than that
Before you entered my life
My body was just a shell
An empty hollow place filled with
Dreams of love
Yet, never having truly experienced it
Then in came you……
You came out of nowhere
And how ironic
I can't imagine my life without you there

My Daughter

I often sit and wonder
If you would have looked like me
Would your smile still
Bring one from me
Would your dimple remain?
If your hair would still
Have been soft as silk
I wonder if your skin
Would have remained as clear
And blessed with no imperfections
I look at your twin
And have to grin
Because my darling if you
Would have been like him
I would have definitely had
To ask the Lord to have mercy upon me
At times I think he is the way
He is to make up for you
And for some reason that
Always seems to warm my soul
You are my daughter,
A daughter I wasn't allowed
To fully know
But never doubt that I loved you wholeheartedly
And I always will
When I close my eyes, I see your image
An image that's embedded within my mind
Heart and soul
The image of my daughter

In Loving Memory of My Beloved Kiara Denise

Dedicated to Mr. Kevonn Demar

As I sit here beside your bed
Thoughts run through my head
Wondering if you will be fine
Baby boy, just to hear you whine
To see you move around, be careful
Not to hit the ground
Many tears I've cried
Many tears I've dried
From my face
You hold a special place
In my heart
Us two will never part
You are a part of me
Oh, can't you see
I need you for me
To be free
From the pain
Look at the rain
As it pours through the drain
Washing with it all of the pain
Washing it all away
Let us pray
I love you baby

Proud of Who You Have Manifested Into… You Have Given Me
Apart of Her to Carry Me Through…...Blessed

Dedicated to Ms. Kiara Denise

Have you ever been empty?
From the loss of a loved one
Or better yet, a child,
Well that emptiness is what I feel
As I put this pen to paper
And I release my deepest emotions
No matter what I do it just feels as if
I'm going through the motions,
Trying to maintain
And deal with the pain
What if this tragedy struck?
Not once but twice?
Was this just an unlucky roll of the dice?
You can't question life
Just roll with the punches
And deal with the strife
I honestly hope that no one can relate
This life I would not wish upon anyone
Because when it's all said and done
You really have no one
So, when times seem hard
Always put your trust in God

Dedicated to Mr. DaQuan Jamique

In a few weeks it will be five years
Since you've past
However, it was only a few days ago
When I thought of you last
You seem to fill my head these days
Your face shining in my mind like
Soft sunrays
For nine months I carried you
I just wish that you knew
How much your mommy really love you

Complete

I've searched a lifetime
To find
The one to make my life complete
Sometimes, I thought it was all in
My mind
And that true love,
I would never find

And now as I gaze
Upon your face
I'm stuck with reality
You have entered my life
To finally take your place
By my side
Walking with me step for step
Only you can reach into the depths
Of my soul
To release the true, me

Blessed

You have changed my life
In so many ways
I still sit back
And remember the days
My life before you
Was filled with pain
My love is like the sun
Willing to come out after the rain
On that wonderful day
You entered my life
I knew you were the one
I had to ask
"Will you be my wife?"
To my surprise you said yes
I thought to myself
Never, have I been so blessed.

www.ingramcontent.com/pod-product-compliance
Lightning Source LLC
Chambersburg PA
CBHW061808050726
47598CB00002B/919